Positive

Go From Nega ... ... *Positive* *and Achieve Happiness and Success for Life*

Harvey Segler

FREE Bonus!

<u>Want to be productive, healthier and more successful?…</u>

Visit >>> www.ProjectSuperPerformance.com <<< to get free tips about healthy foods, productivity strategies and other nice tricks for a happier, better and more productive life.

At the moment you can get a FREE download of:

"33.5 Power Habits That Will Change Your Life"

But hurry up, the book will not be there forever!

Visit This Website And Download It Now! 100% Free! What Do You Have To Lose?!

If you don't want the book, read the blog which can teach you who wants to be a super performer at work, as a parent, in school or maybe as an athlete how to be just that.

Introduction

I want to thank you and congratulate you for downloading the book, *Positive Thinking*.

This book contains proven steps and strategies on how to rid your life of all the negative thinking and destructive influences that do nothing but bring you down.

We all want to be happy in life, and as a general rule of thumb we do what we can to make our lives happy. We go to extremes to do things that will hopefully make us happy, whether it be buying things, going on exotic trips all over the world, dating, working, or whatever it may be, mankind is on a constant trek to gain happiness.

If you stop for a second and really give it some thought, you will see that I am right. Everything we do and say is for the hopeful end result that we will then be happy with our lives.

It is in our DNA. From birth, our focus in on being happy. We know what we want, even from a very young age, and we cry when we don't get it. When we finally do get what we were after, we stop.

It is something that we just automatically do, and the drive for happiness is something that pushes us through nearly all of our life decisions.

Maybe if we made more money we would be happy. Or maybe if we had more friends, maybe if you looked like that person or lost 5 pounds, then you would be happy.

Maybe if you were different, or if you were someone else. Or maybe you can pin your unhappiness on what someone else did to you when you were younger. If they hadn't bothered you or butted in where they didn't belong, you would be happy today.

I hate to be the one to say it, but ultimately those things have nothing to do with how happy you are. That is why you see people who are simply stunning to look at, have more money than they know what to do with, and all the comforts that you long for, yet they are still not happy.

No matter what, if we are not sure of what makes us happy, or know how to make ourselves happy, we are never going to achieve that happiness. We think that it is impossible for us to be unhappy if we get that one thing that we have been longing for, but we don't stop to think of how it always works out in the end.

We refuse to look back over our lives and think of the things that we thought would make us happy before. We saved and saved as a kid to get that one thing, or we refuse to think of how we just thought that the one person we wanted to date was going to be the answer to our happiness.

Now you know that none of those things were able to make you happy, but you are insistent that there are still other things out there that eventually will. Sure, you may not have found that thing yet, but you keep telling yourself that if you buy this one thing or that other thing then you are going to hit the magic button of happiness and never have to deal with anything that is sad again.

The denial of this fact is what fuels your life as you strive to find that one thing that is going to make you happy, and refuse to believe that it's not out there.

What makes this seem even bleaker is the fact that there is no magic formula for happiness, you can't ever make the right number of anything to ensure you will be happy tomorrow. The newness wears off of any new relationship, things get old and break.

Even after a long vacation you have to deal with the stress of going back to work, figure out what you missed, what you need to do now, and how you are going to pay for everything you did when you were out and about in the world. And after all of this dies down, you start to feel overwhelmed about your life once again, then it isn't long before you are hoping to go on another vacation.

The same goes for the rest of the things that we spend our days pursuing, we are always working on what we can have next, and what will make us happy then. We look around at our coworkers and we are convinced that they are happy because of things such as where they live or how much they are making.

Or maybe it is what they are driving or who they are dating that is making them happy. Whatever the reason for their happiness, we have ourselves convinced that we are going to be happy if we get the same things that they have.

After all, that is where happiness comes from, isn't it?

But this can't be it. There are a lot of happy people out there. Chances are, you know a few of them. They are those people that just go about life, and no matter what their situation is, they seem to be happy.

There doesn't seem to be a thing on this planet that is able to shake them. They are clearly the 'glass is always half-full' types, and it doesn't seem to matter if it is hot, cold, windy, rainy, sunny, or anything.

They can be dealing with the unthinkable in their lives, or they could be running on cloud nine all the time, with life handed to them in a gift wrapped package. There are times you think you can blame your unhappiness and their happiness on what they are doing or given, but then you realize there are those that may be unwell or dealing with tragedy and they are still happy.

In fact, they may be dressed well, dressed poorly, rich, poor, struggling... who knows? Yet they always seem to be happy. It is almost as if you can't bring them down even if you tried.

Of course there are the other people in the world, too. Those that have everything handed to them, and have the most cushioned life that someone could ask for, yet nothing is ever good enough. They manage to find fault in everything, even if it is something they thought they wanted.

You like to ignore these people, or blame their unhappiness on the fact that they don't have this or that they say they want, but you can't bring yourself to say that they are unhappy because of anything beyond they don't have what they want.

You medicate and justify your need to have more things because you tell yourself that even those that are rich and pampered still need to have more things in order to be happy.

These people are everywhere, but they don't seem to have the same power as the positive thinkers. Those that are positive just seem to rise above the crowd and do their own thing, and not let themselves be bothered by what is going on with the rest of the world.

So what is their secret? How did they manage to reach this level of happiness, and is there a way you can get it for yourself? Do you have to be some sort of superhero to feel happy that often, or is there really something simple that you can learn to do that will help you to also be that happy?

Does it help to expose yourself to all kinds of sunlight, and drink magic drinks, and wear bracelets or rubber bands that will make you feel happier a lot better? Or maybe you are one of those that spends all of your days reading those motivational quotes and energizing yourself.

It would be so much easier if you were like the people that made the motivational quotes, and if you were just happy because you were, so you didn't have to worry about what you did or what you bought.

But what is their secret? How do they do it? Is there something different about them that makes them happier than you?

Don't worry, these people are not superheroes, they have just figured out what it means to think positively. Positive thinking is powerful, and it changes how you view every aspect of your life.

No matter what you may be going through, there is always a reason to be happy, and thinking positively will help you achieve that. It may sound trite, or to some who are going through a lot of bad things in their lives, it may seem to be insensitive, but it isn't.

We are designed to be happy people, and we are supposed to gravitate towards things that make us happy. There is nothing more spiritual, more mature, or anything like that. It is not wrong or disrespectful to be happy, it is what we are designed to be.

By the time you reach the end of this book, you will be able to:

- Think positively no matter what your situation is

- Find the good in everything

- Look up, and not down, when bad things happen

- And learn to apply this thinking to every aspect of your life

No matter who you are or what you have been through, you will be able to also learn the art of positive thinking, and in no time at all you will notice a drastic… and positive… difference start to take root in your own life.

This is going to be a journey of acceptance, and of personal growth. You are not going to feel bad about your happiness, and you are going to be a lot better off when you know that you are ok with being happy.

You don't ever have to feel bad about your happiness, and you need to give yourself permission right now to be happy. Make sure that you are open to learning and open to accepting your happiness.

Positive thinking is acquired like a new taste. You may have to take some time to learn how to use your newfound way of thinking, but you will be glad when you master this ability and it becomes second nature.

So what are you waiting for? There is a life of positive out there, just waiting for you to join in.

Thanks again for downloading this book, I hope you enjoy it!

Table of contents

held against the publisher for any reparation, damages, or monetary loss due to the information herein, either directly or indirectly.

Respective authors own all copyrights not held by the publisher.

The information herein is offered for informational purposes solely, and is universal as so. The presentation of the information is without contract or any type of guarantee assurance.

The trademarks that are used are without any consent, and the publication of the trademark is without permission or backing by the trademark owner. All trademarks and brands within this book are for clarifying purposes only and are the owned by the owners themselves, not affiliated with this document.

Chapter 1 – Learning to See the Good

It would be a lie to tell you that positivity comes easily to everyone. There are a lot of people out there that are struggling with a number of different problems, whether they be financial, relationship, or otherwise.

They do what they can to get ahead, and to see the best, but they always slip back into depression and seeing the worst in things. As we have said before, it is something that we are all naturally seeking, but it is not something that we all come by naturally.

Just the opposite, in fact. We as people tend to see the worst in situations, and see that thing are going wrong. We like to focus on the bad, and feel sorry for ourselves. Even if we deny that and say that we want it to be something good, there is a part of us that gets pleasure out of feeling sorry for ourselves.

You may be one of those people, someone who is tired of the struggle, tired of trying to be happy when you feel like it is all hopeless, tired of trying to be the glue to keep it all together.

Just, tired.

You are exhausted, but you are also expected to be happy and upbeat, at least to look like you are. You are supposed to show up to work with a smile, say hello to everyone that you cross paths with, and act like you are completely fine when you may be someone who is struggling to keep it together at all.

No one understands how you feel better than we do. Everyone goes through troubles and trials, but there are some who are able to withstand even the most unthinkable problems, yet come out smiling on the other side.

These people aren't some sort of super person, or anyone that has anything better going on for them than you do. What these people do have is the ability to think positively, even when they are under incredible pain or pressure.

Now, no one said that this was going to be easy. You have to first learn how to think this way, and you have to put it into deliberate practice before you are able to have it come to you naturally.

We are not stuck in our thought patterns. We are able to control how we think and feel about things, especially when we are making a deliberate effort to do so. It is a foreign concept to most that they have a say in this.

Many people think that they are a victim of society and circumstance. They think that they are just walking around on this planet, and that they are left to hope for the best.

If they aren't that lucky, bad things happen to them, and they are left feeling like all they can do is keep it together and wallow in their misery. There is no feeling that there is ever going to be anything better, and all they can do is hope to make it through to the next situation.

We have an entire society that feels this way; that is why those that are not negative in their thinking are those that seem so out of the ordinary. When you see a person that is not so consumed with negative thinking that they are able to be happy in spite of their circumstances, they seem to be really out of the ordinary.

But there is nothing predisposed about these people, they have just learned how to see the positive in life.

That being said, at first, it is a choice. Now, maybe this is not what you want to hear right now, or maybe it is not what you feel like you can hear right now. We have no idea what you may be going through, and telling a person that it is a choice to think positively comes off as rather condescending to those that are in the midst of pain or depression.

Let me assure you of this, however, while it is a conscious action you have to make at first, it is not something that will take very long to take root. Our minds and bodies were designed to pursue the positive.

It is a simple fact of nature: we like to be happy. As we saw before, most everything that we do is in a quest to be happy.

When depression takes root, it is not because you prefer to be sad, it just becomes easier to be sad than happy. It's like a heavy cape that you have to shake off, but when you do, you will be able to see clearly how you can be happy as a habit of life.

We could break it down to the chemical methods that take place in your brain, but we won't bore you with all those details. What matters is that you have an understanding of what is taking place, and that you can change it.

There is nothing that happens in your life that you can't change. Sure, there are things that you can't change that happen in your life, but you can always change how you are feeling, and what you can do to in response to what happened to you.

It is no secret that there are rough things that happen to everyone. I am not going to undermine anything that has happened to you, or that may happen to you, but I do want to encourage you to look for the positive in those things, and follow the steps in this book to achieve that happiness.

I don't want to make it sound like this is easy, it can be hard enough to hear that you need to make the conscious choice to make this happen, but I do want you to know that you are able to make this change.

You are a strong person, and you are able to make this change, what is important that you actually make the change. Power to make a change, is an amazing thing, and that in and of itself is enough to make you feel like you are able to get to where you need to be.

People who know how to be positive are aware of this power, and that is something that you have to keep in mind as you strive to become one yourself.

That is another thing you have to remember about positive people. Positive people may be happy go lucky kind of people, but that doesn't mean that they are always happy.

You can be a perfectly positive person, and still feel sad inside. Sadness is an emotion, just like the rest of your emotions, and it is, in fact, really healthy to let it out in times it comes up, but we will discuss more on that later.

And another thing that you should keep in mind is that you can be a positive person but not have that happy go lucky outlook on life. There are so many different personalities on this planet, and you are going to have your own, regardless of whether or not you are positive.

If you are a quiet and reserved human being, then you are going to be that way no matter what you are feeling on the inside. It is a misdirection to tell people that they have to be outgoing and enthusiastic in order to be a positive person, because that is not the case at all.

You can be a perfectly happy and positive person, and you will still be quiet and like to keep to yourself as much as possible. What is even more important than that is to remember that feeling like you want to be reserved is also perfectly fine. There is nothing at all wrong with a person who likes to keep to themselves, and positivity is for yourself, anyway.

All of that is rather a side note, however, and we don't want to get away from the main point of what we are talking about.

Right now, we are going to focus on the fact that you can be positive and be really happy, but you can also be positive and feel sad. It isn't the emotion that you feel that defines whether you are a positive person in life, it is how you view life itself.

Do you feel that this is all crashing down, and that there is no hope for anyone? Do you think it is pointless to look for the good in life because there is so much bad?

If so, you are not engaging in positive thinking. Positive thinkers do acknowledge that bad things happen in life. That is just a part of the world we live in. What positive thinkers don't do is feel like we are all doomed, or that this is all going nowhere.

It is a completely different outlook on a given situation, and it has nothing to do with the situations that they are in. you can be a positive person and have the worst luck in the world, or you can be a negative person and have everything good happening to you.

What matters is how you are going to handle sadness. As we have already said, it is something that happens to everyone, and it is natural, and healthy, to allow yourself to feel that way from time to time.

When being sad becomes a problem is when you are feeling sad and letting it take root in your life, and turning into a depression. There is a vast difference between sadness and depression, and the heart of the issue is where this difference lies. Sure, you can be sad that something happens, but you don't have to let it define who you are or what is happening to you.

Positive thinkers have gotten this concept all figured out. Now, I am not going to say that they have their lives figured out, or that they are able to handle things just the right way, but what I am saying is that their overall outlook on life is figured out.

They know that no matter what happens, there is a good coming, and ultimately that good is going to win out. Sure, there may be a lot of pain right now, but that doesn't mean it is going to last forever.

To be a positive thinker, you need to realize and acknowledge that bad things do and will happen in life, but that there is going to be a better time coming. Positivity knows that no matter how bad it gets, it is going to be better.

This isn't really something that we can tell you how to do, besides telling you to make the choice to be positive. There are going to be things that happen to you that are not good, and there are going to be things that happen outside of your control.

You have every control over your response, however, and you can choose to view life in a positive light. I am going to give you a bit of a challenge, and that is to think positive the very next time something bad happens to you.

This doesn't have to be anything major, in fact it may be easier to start with things that are on the smaller side.

What you need to do is find the bright. Consider this example. You have a long day at work, you get home, and you find that someone backed their car into your mailbox.

That is annoying enough, but then you get your mail, and you take it inside. That is when you open your bills, and you find that you forgot to pay your bill last month, and now you are getting a fee for it.

Now, you have a couple of choices, and that is to either be positive about it, or to turn to negativity. The first response in this situation for most people is to be disappointed, as you well should be. There are things that happen that are disappointing, and you are going to have to deal with some rough things because of it.

That is not negative, that is an emotion, now, here is where your choice becomes very real, and that is the difference between negative and positive thinkers. When you are debating what to do in this, you need to think about how you are going to view how this affects the rest of your life.

Sure, you can get upset, have a fit, and think that all of the world is against you and nothing is ever going to work out in your favor. Perhaps you are just going to add this to the list of things that have gone wrong this week, and you now have a bunch more to deal with.

That is negative thinking. This is because you are focusing on these things happening to you as your defining points in life. Because those things happened, you are now going to be a failure in life, and you are not going to have anything good happen to you. Or you think that if something else good does, then it will also be taken away from you.

Then there is the choice of positive thinking, and that has a lot different of an outlook. You can see that your mailbox is broken, and you can be glad that it wasn't your house that got hit, or your car.

You can assume that it can be fixed, or that you can get another one. Sure, it isn't the best situation to happen in the world, but it also isn't the end of the world. You can look at your late bills and think about it the same way.

At least you have the money to get it taken care of now, or even if you don't, you know that you will get it taken care of eventually. Think of the donkey in the Winnie the Pooh series, and imagine how he deals with things. That character is largely a negative thinker, and you don't want to be like him.

Focus on what you can control, and the good that can come out of that. Don't worry about the extra things that happen, and don't worry when you feel like everything is going wrong at once.

Sure, they may all feel so heave on your shoulders, but that is not the defining point of your life, and you will find that when you break out of that kind of thinking, that you can then make a difference in how you view the complete outlook of your life.

Look up, even if you have to look a long way to get there. A positive thinker is not a person that thinks that they will never have bad things happen to them, a positive thinker is a person that knows that even when they do, that it will get better eventually.

Watching for that streak of light beside the storm clouds, that is positive thinking.

Chapter 2 – Making Your Own Good in a Sea of Bad

Now that we have looked at the fact positive thinkers acknowledge the bad, let's take a look at how they overcome it. We would be downright delusional to think that if we were to always see the positive, then no bad would happen, but that is just plain old denial.

Positive thinkers accept that bad things happen to them for no reason at all.

There is a common mistake that people make, and that is the mistake of thinking that they are being punished if something bad happens to them. There they are, going about their lives, when something out of the blue hits them.

It could come in many forms, loss of employment, a breakup, a tragedy, money problems, whatever it may be, they have been completely blindsided by it. To make matters worse, they not only have to deal with whatever just happened to them, they feel that they must have done something bad to deserve this horrible trial.

Now, they may not be able to determine what it is that they did to deserve such a thing, or they may pull things from their past that happened so far back then that you question how they are able to remember it at all. Then there are those that make up a reason that they deserve to be punished, and you have to wonder why they feel that they screwed up so bad.

I am sure you are able to relate to this kind of thinking, even if it is just a small scale. Have you ever gotten a speeding ticket or a parking ticket, and assumed it happened to you because you complained about how someone else was behaving the day before?
Or have you figured that since you lied about what happened the other night at the party, that is why you are now dealing with your favorite jeans being all ripped up?

These are just examples, but to many, they are able to relate to some extent. They think that they are going to be punished for all kinds of things, even if that is completely out of the blue. Now don't get me wrong, I am not saying that it is ok for you to do those things to other people, and that there are still other things that can happen when you do make mistakes, but what I am saying, is that you are not being punished.

I am here to tell you that is not true. Bad things happen to good people, it's a fact of life. No matter who you are, what you do, or what you think, you are going to have good days and bad.

That's just the way it is.

We live in a world where bad things happen. They happen to good people and they happen to bad people, the effects of these bad things that happen are completely random, and they can hit any person at any given moment.

Now some feel that is not fair, and they don't want to accept this kind of thinking because it takes away from their control in life. That is a hard thing for some people to accept. They want to be in control, and if they can think that they are being punished for some reason, then they are the ones who brought it down on themselves.

People like to be in control. It is hard to give up this control, because for many it makes them feel small and helpless, and like they are sitting on a time bomb that is about to go off and shower all kinds of bad things down on top of them. I am not saying that it is easy to give up this control, but what I am saying is that you can do it, and that it is actually beneficial to your growth.

When you have to accept that bad things happen just because, it is a lot harder to imagine that you are not in control of your own life, and for some people, that is a very scary thought to come to terms with.

When you are letting go, you are able to free yourself more and become more positive in your thinking. This is an art that you need to learn how to do. Don't automatically assume the worst when a bad thing happens, just like you can't assume that it is going to turn out bad in the end.

There are many forms of negative thinking, and some of those forms come in the manner of thinking that it is all your fault. Let go of that, and understand that it isn't your fault. Take responsibility when you need to, and make sure you are living a good and moral life, but don't assume that every little bad thing that happens is a direct result of you not brushing your teeth the night before.

Now, to be a positive thinker, you are not going to let this fact get you down. Yes, we have bad days, but we also have good. To take it a step further, think of how the bad days make you appreciate the good days that much more.

Just because something bad is happening to you, that doesn't mean you are a bad person, and it doesn't mean you have done something wrong, all it means is that you are a human, living on a world where bad things happen. Just remember, even when you are in the thick of it, there is a better day on the horizon, and if you stick this out, you will be there in no time.

I am not saying that it won't be hard now, and that it will be over quickly, but what I am telling you is that you are strong enough to make it through, and if you are consistent, and willing to make the effort to see the good in things, then you are going to make it through in the long run, and come out on the other side a stronger and happier person.

Positive thinkers don't dwell on the bad things that happen to them.

Complaining and whining have become as common if not more common to you then smiles. It seems that more people than not are more than happy to sit you down and tell you why life has dealt them a bad hand.

It can be easy to get sucked into this kind of thinking, and even easier to get it stuck in your speech. We all like to sit around and talk about the bad that has happened to us. We thrive on that drama. If you don't believe, me, consider this:

If you are feeling sorry for yourself, you don't usually sit by and keep it to yourself. No, you want to tell someone, let them feel sorry for you and with you, and you want to let it be known that you are going through a difficult time.

You may have different reasons for doing this, whether it be because you like the attention, you like to have people feel sorry for you, and you like to be in the center of attention, but you need to break out of this line of thinking if you are going to set this aside for good.

When we are feeling sorry for ourselves, we tend to blow things out of proportion, and make them a lot worse than they really are. It doesn't matter to us what it is that is causing our distress, we just want others to know that we are feeling that way, and that we don't deserve that kind of treatment from the world.

And, you will also take note, that it doesn't matter what you are complaining about, as long as you have something to complain about. Even if you are having the greatest day there is, there are still things that can happen that will give you a reason to complain, and more often than not, you are apt to take the opportunity.

Bills, family, friends, whatever the case may be, they are not being treated as they should be. Or maybe it is something that is completely out of their control, and they whine about the weather.

We all know that person who never has a nice thing to say about anyone, and rarely is having a good day. Even on the nicest of days when they are given all kinds of things to be grateful for, they still spend their days griping and whining that not all is well in their world.

Close your eyes, right now, and picture that person. Is it you? Many of us think of someone else right away, but if we are really open with ourselves, we can likely pinpoint that we are that same person.

We act like we are happy to see a person to their face, then when they turn their back, we are more than happy to gripe about them to whoever will listen.

But why is this? Why do we and so many other people feel the need to gripe and whine about other people and outside circumstances when they are just as capable of being happy and seeing the positive?

It takes just as much effort to say something bad as it does to say something good, and it is just as easy to talk about things that are good and uplifting.

The problem is, they are only focusing on the bad. It is something they have done for so long, it is what they have trained their brains to do. Now, even when something good happens to them, they automatically assume that it's not going to last, or that is isn't as good as it could be.

When you are first trying to train your brain to be positive, these are the people that you want to avoid. This may be difficult if you have to work with them, or if you live with them, but it is possible.

Don't think that you can stay strong and positive and still hang around them, they are going to be poison to you, and you are not able to withstand it in your early stages. Don't believe me? Think of it this way.

When you are starting a new diet, or when you are trying to quit drinking, you are not going to go to the bar or to a buffet. You are not going to be hanging around with your friends that are all about that kind of life, and you are going to try to hang out with people that live more like those you want to live like.

Negative thinking is just as bad of a habit as drinking and overeating, and it has just as bad of an effect on your health. It is true that those who are negative in their day to day lives are those that are more likely to suffer all kinds of illness and other issues with their health.

Just think of your own life, and how you feel when you are stressed out. You feel like you are sick, your stomach hurts, and you feel tired. This is also what negative thinking will do to you.

It will creep in, and you will have that level of tiredness creep into your brain, and you won't be able to shake it. It will feel like you need to lie down and rest when you haven't been doing anything strenuous. You may start to border on depression, and you may start to feel like you are slipping into sadness.

What is so destructive about this is that like attracts like, and you will find that those that are negative are going to want you to stay negative with them. They won't be happy that you are going to be more positive, and they will do what they can to keep you the same as them.

This may sound silly to you at first, but you have to think about it. When you are stuck in this kind of thinking, you are going to be more comfortable with others that are also like you. You don't want one of your own to branch out and change, because that will mean that they will be different, and you won't have anyone to gripe with anymore.

You need to stay away from these people as much as you can, and if you can, you should replace them entirely with new friends. Now, I am not saying that you need to get rid of your friends, or that you shouldn't speak with them anymore, but what I am saying is that you should consider taking some time to regroup and find what it is you are wanting in life, and work on from there.

You know right now that you want to be more positive, and that isn't going to happen if you are spending all of your time with negative people, so you need to make sure that you avoid them as often as you can.

Even if you can't stay away from them all together, you can stay away from their negative conversations. It is all too easy to get sucked into negative thinking, and for a newly positive mind, you don't want to do anything that will suffocate it out of you.

If you are at work, and all of your coworkers are negative, it is hard to stay away from them, but you don't have to participate in their negative conversations. You can stay away from them on break, or you can try to change the subject when it turns south.

You don't have to participate in a conversation that you don't like, and you can always say something positive instead. It is a major temptation to get stuck with them in the rut of negativity, but I promise you that you can break out of it if you are willing to put in the time and effort to do so.

It is so simple, that I challenge you to try it tomorrow. You may not be able to do it all right away, but you can make a start at it. If you are a person that has struggled with these kinds of thoughts, then you may need to take the new outlook in small doses.

There are those that are able to make a change right away, and they make it and never look back. When you are doing this kind of change, you need to make sure that you are taking this in amounts that you are able to keep up with.

There are going to be times that means that you need to make a conscious effort to make the change that you want to see.

Sometimes you have to look for the positive.

There are going to be times in your life when the positive may not be completely evident at first. These are the times when you have to be careful that you don't get sucked into negative thinking.

When you are breaking out of this, you might need to do things that are active and capable of making that change in you. Don't just think about how you want to do it, actually get out there and do it. Do whatever it takes to make yourself see the positive in your situation, even if that means that you need to sit down and make a list.

Another thing you can do is compare what you have to those who have nothing. There are all kinds of charity organizations that are out there, and just looking at them you can see that you have a lot of things that they don't. This shouldn't make you feel like better than them, but it should make you feel grateful.

Gratefulness is a great place to start when you are trying to think more positively. When you think about how much you have, and how much you are given, you will see that you aren't as bad off as you think you are.

I am not saying that it isn't hard, in fact, when you are in the middle of an issue, that is when you feel the most negative, and when you feel the most like giving up.

If you are going through something, and you aren't seeing the positive, start listing things that have nothing to do with that situation, and focus on those. For example, if you are struggling with money issues, remind yourself that you are healthy at least.

If you are sick, remind yourself that you have food, clothes, and means to get well again.

If you really can't seem to think of anything that is positive, simply think about the fact you are alive, and focus on how good that feels. Even when everything comes crashing down, there are the most basic things to be positive about.

It is a crazy thing, this gift of life, and all too many of us tend to forget that we are lucky to be alive. We are lucky to be in a world that we are in, with all of its beautiful sights and sounds, and we are lucky to live in the day and age that we live in.

All things considering, we are living in an incredible time in this world, and it is hard to imagine what life would be like in a different timeframe. Be grateful for whatever you can think of, and you will see that you have a lot of things to be grateful for.

This isn't something that is going to happen to you overnight. In fact, it does take deliberate practice to get to the point that you actually start to feel positive in many different kinds of situations, but I promise you, that with consistency, you will be able to learn how to be positive in any situation.

Now, don't misunderstand, there are going to be a lot of times in your life when you are sad, and while we can all hope that we never have to face tragedy or anything like that in our lives, you do have to realize that there is a chance that you will have to at some point.

This isn't going to undermine what you are going through, and it is not disrespectful to be positive even when the world is crashing down around you. You don't need to be happy, and you shouldn't be hard on yourself when you aren't.

There are times in life when it is ok to be sad, but you should always remember that it is going to be ok at the end.

Chapter 3 – Positive Energy

There is a lot of good that comes from being positive, and some of that even spills into the physical realm.

The mind is a powerful instrument. Your thoughts control so much of what you feel, even those subconscious feelings that you don't pay much mind to. If you are a negative person, you will find that there is an actual physical difference in your day than if you were not.

Negative people often feel tired, irritable, and fall sick often. Headaches are common, and so are other aches and pains. Now, this may seem strange if you think about it, but really, the body responds to the outlook the person has on life.

The yin yang mindset.

Your health hinges so much on your emotional wellbeing, it's almost frightening. There are so many ways you can negatively impact your health just by negative thinking patterns.

Stress is a number one cause of disease in the United States, and it has major negative impact worldwide. While some stress is good for you, the stress that comes out of a negative mindset could prove to be deadly.

Now, we are not talking about stress in and of itself. Just like sadness, there is a healthy level of stress that you should have in your life. It doesn't have to be every day, and it doesn't have to be a certain kind of stress, but you do need to realize that it is going to be there.

A positive person isn't immune to stress, they merely know how to handle their stress. They don't dwell on things that make it worse, but instead they start to think of the things that make them feel happy.

This is sort of along the same lines as acknowledging that there are bad things that happen in this world. You can be a perfectly positive person, and you may have to deal with a lot of stress in your day.

This could be the good kind of stress that comes out of a demanding job, or it can be the bad kind of stress that comes out of difficult relationships, money problems, and other kinds of things that can be really harmful to you. Positive people can experience all kinds of stress, good and bad.

There is a perfect balance to the world. Good and bad, positive and negative. You need to learn how to balance these two things in your own life. Let the bad things come and go as they please, but don't ever get caught up in them, or allow them to affect your life negatively.

When you view every moment as passing, you will take greater care to appreciate the good ones, and you will notice that the bad ones don't seem to be that bad anymore.

Don't get so wrapped up in the positive mindset that you turn into something that you aren't. I know that sounds funny in a book that is all about positive thinking, but you have to bear with me here, and I will explain further what I mean.

This is a world of balance, and if you are so stressed out you are not being a part of that balance. Of course, you can expect me to leave it at that, and have that be the lesson here, but that isn't my point.

When you are super positive, you may not allow yourself to experience the other emotions that come from living on this planet. That means that you need to keep it in balance. Remember that you are human, and you have all kinds of emotions. Keep your negative in check, but also keep a balance with your positive.

We are striving for that perfect balance, and hoping for one that you can live with all your life. This of course is going to take a lot of practice, but you have to remember that anything worth doing is worth the work involved.

Just remember, for every negative there is a positive, and for every positive, there are even more positives to be found.

Positive thoughts spread like wildfire.

A person who make a habit out of positive thinking will soon realize that it doesn't take much and their positive thoughts turn into more positive thoughts. It isn't as though for every positive there is a negative you have to beat out of your mind, no! For every positive thought you have, your brain is that much more inclined to make more positive thoughts.

We are highly trainable creatures. This is true in a variety of aspects, including positive thinking. When you are training your mind, you need to remember that there are a lot of things that you can do to make it better, but also to make it not react as you would like it to.

If you train your mind to automatically assume one thing when you are feeling another, that can be good, but if you are getting stuck in denial, that is bad. Strike that balance here, and let your positive thoughts come forth as much as you possibly can.

Don't think that you are doing it wrong if it takes some time for it to become a habit for you, this sort of thing takes time no matter who you are or what you are doing, what is important is that you realize that you need to work on it, and that the more you do the more progress you are going to see.

The good thing about this kind of training is that you get to see the results of it almost immediately. When you see the progress starting, you will be more apt to try it again. You will also notice that your positivity will bring in more people who are positive, and it will be easier to find more people like yourself.

Your body will be positively affected when you think this way as well. Of course there are still positive people who are sick with horrible illnesses, but it is a proven fact that thinking good thoughts and having a good attitude on life will help your body deal with illness so much better than a person who does not share these thoughts.
Why?

Because your body feeds off of the brain. There are so many chemicals and signals the brain gives off every single minute of every day, and when it is giving off signals of pain and sorrow, the rest of your body is sure to feel the effects.

This doesn't mean that you will never get sick if you are positive, it merely means that you are better able to deal with your illness, and you will be more likely to have a stronger recovery if you are looking for the good in life.

You will also notice that other people's attitudes feed off of your own. You may not realize how much influence you have in your life, until you try something like this. Whether you are dealing with a lot of people in a day, or if you are dealing with only one, your attitude does have an effect on theirs.

This can be good or bad, depending on how you are using your privilege here. Is isn't really up to you to make or break their day, but you can make their attitude a lot better, or you can make them have to fight to have a good attitude by the way that you treat them.

Habits hold stronger than you think.

All this really comes down to is a matter of habits. How you think about things... including life in general, will be manifested in ways that you can't even begin to imagine.

There are all kinds of habits that we already do in our day. We get up, we brush our teeth, we do our chores and go about our day. There are few things that come into our day that are outside the norm, and we really come to appreciate the norm for what it is.

There are many people that don't like the word, habit. They think that it means something bad, and they would rather avoid it, but that is just silly. Habits can be good or bad, depending on what they are, and the more good habits we can get into your day, the more the bad habits are going to go away.

Your health is affected on so many levels by your attitudes, and your very emotional baseline is a direct result of your thoughts and reactions to things that happen in your day. Don't ever let things get to you to the extent they harm your health. Once that is gone, there is no telling how long it will take to get it back.

So how do we begin with our new habit? Well, we have been talking about that a lot so far, but there are always ways we can touch on it more so you know what it is you should be doing to get to where you want to be.

First of all, it is important to identify what it is you are doing in your day already. Sure, you may know that you are not as positive as you want to be, but that isn't enough to make sure that you are going to be getting out of your negative habit. What you want to do is sit down and look at your day, and see where the negativity is creeping in.

Just as you would sit down and see when you were starting to drink, or sit down and think about where your diet started to go south, you should sit down and see when you are starting to go negative with your day.

Is it in the morning, when you decide that you are going to update your Facebook? What is it you say when you get on first thing in the morning? Are you glad to be on and greet the new day, or are you griping that it is something with the day that you don't like?

Maybe it is when you get to work, and you feel that you can't be positive there, because no one else is. When does it start? When you bid each other good day, or when you start to talk about the weekend?

There is always a start. That is what you need to remember. When you wake up in the morning, you are a blank canvas. You haven't spoken to anyone, and you haven't said anything to yourself that is negative.

Sure, you may be thinking things that aren't so positive, but that can be remedied easier than when you are talking about it all the time.

Once you have figured out where your negativity starts, that is when you can change it. And the method is simple, all you have to do is change. Don't say something negative, and don't let them turn your conversation to the negative.

Be positive whenever you can, even if you are doing something so trivial as updating your social media. You would be surprised at where these habits like to sneak in, and where we are most apt to use them without even thinking about it.

When we are looking to get attention or approval, that is when it is the worst, but that, too, is thinking that we need to get changed. Why do we think that we need to be negative in order to get attention? There are all kinds of things that we can do that will help us get the attention of others, so why go with something that is so destructive as negativity?

Now, as with any habit, we like to see progress in our efforts to quit. When you are trying to quit this habit, it may help you to keep a calendar and see where you are and how much progress you have been making.

It is a positive thing for you to get into the notes, and see where you were then, and where you are now. The positive side of you is going to tell you that you are doing a good job, even when it is day 1, or 2, or 3... as long as you are moving forward, you can see how you are doing a good thing for yourself, and you will be motivated to keep it going.

They say that it takes about three weeks to break a habit, but we need to do more than just break that habit, we need to replace it with something new, and that it why you should make sure you are keeping track of all of this.

They say it takes a matter of weeks to form a new habit, so you really have no time to waste. You can start to think of positive things right now, and you will be amazed at how easy it starts to come to you, no matter what you are faced with in your day.

Chapter 4 – Party of One

One thing you have to realize, is there are a handful of positive thinkers in a sea full of negativity. There are going to be many, many times in your life when you are the only person with a good attitude in a given situation.

Don't be afraid to stand alone.

It is of utmost importance that you don't be afraid to stand alone in these situations. Whether it be negativity as a result of bad attitudes, or negativity as a result of a literal emergency, turning negative yourself will never solve anything, it will only make the problem worse.

You have seen this portrayed over and over in Hollywood movies, and you more likely than not get annoyed at the person in the film that is starting to freak out after they have been the one that was so firm and strong on the outset.

You can see that they have been doing a good job of keeping it all together, then you will see that they are starting to fade. Sure, you may not think much of this at first, but by the time they crack and turn into everyone else, you are disappointed, but what makes matters worse is that you could be doing the same exact thing if you are not careful.

Let's put all of this in perspective. It is easy to point the finger when we are thinking that it is all about someone else, but the world takes on a whole new meaning when we are faced with the same kind of situation in our own lives.

For example, if it is a long, hot day at work, and all you want to do is go home, it won't make the day pass any faster if you join in the complaining. On the flip side of that, don't get drawn into the complaining just because someone else is doing it.

There are other things that you can say that will make the situation seem less negative, but you have to remember that there are people that are good at what they do. And if that is negativity, then your positivity could be up for a run.

Don't be afraid to stand up for yourself, but at the same time, don't get drawn in when it is silly and you don't need to prove a point. There are a lot of times when it is ok to be silent, and you don't have to say anything at all.

Who cares if everyone is hot and tired, you are, they are, we are all aware that everyone else is, so why sit around and talk about it? Why don't you just buckle down and get your work done so you can all go home?

That seems like it would be easy to do right now, but when you are in there, and when you are in the thick of it, it can be a lot harder to be the one that is positive.

Make sure that you are doing what you can to bring the positive to the rest of the world, and understand that this may mean that you don't say anything at all sometimes. There is nothing wrong with silence, and you can be assured that it will go better in any situation to not say anything at all than to say something and hope that you don't get put down or made fun of.

Misery loves company, and without even realizing it, the negative influence may be pressuring you, too, to be negative for the plain and simple fact they are. It is times like these when you have to be bold enough to stand alone in your thinking.

You don't have to give any kind of speech, or say anything at all to the person who is being negative if you don't want to, all you have to do is stay positive yourself.

You will find that more often than not, you are going to get ignored, so this is going to be a journey that could potentially be rather lonely at first, but you have to realize that once the initial hardship is over, it is going to get a lot easier to do.

This really does become second nature to anyone who is doing it, and you will find that there are those that will start to look up to you and wish they were more like you when it comes to being positive.

But what if you have to join in with a conversation?

Of course there are times when you will get dragged into conversations that have a negative twist to them, whether you want to or not. With so much negativity in the world it's hard to avoid it, if not impossible.

This can be especially true if you are only working with a couple of people, if you are living with a negative person, or if your boss is someone who is negative. You may not want to talk that way, but there are going to be times when it is unavoidable.

You don't have to worry about these conversations, and you don't have to dread when they take place, but what you do need to do is be prepared. Everything in life tends to go better when you have a plan, even if it is just a loose plan that will make you have a rough idea of what you should do next.

No one said that anything had to be set in stone, but what you do have to remember is that when you have at least a rough idea of what you are shooting for, you won't be left speechless or even worse, get drawn into the negativity.

So what do you do if you are dragged in? Acknowledge but don't condone. You can say things like "I'm sorry you feel this way," or "I'm sorry you are so uncomfortable," but you don't have to join in with the complaining.

It may even do some good to offer to help them out. Ask if you can do anything to give them a hand in their hardship, you may find it surprising that more often than not the person who is complaining will tell you that they have it handled, they were 'just saying.'

As funny as it is, you are going to run into this more and more as you strive to stay positive in your speech. You do have to remember, however, that there isn't anything that anyone can do that can change your outlook on life.

Sure, these people may think that they have a bad card dealt to them in life, but what they are really looking for is a chance to be negative, and you happen to be the person who was standing there.

But that raises the question of 'why?' Why would you do something to bring down the rest of the people there because you felt like complaining? It didn't get the complainer anywhere by complaining, and they didn't even want help out of their situation. This is a shining example of negativity at its finest.

Always wanting to be heard, but never wanting to actually feel better.

This shouldn't come as any surprise to you, you know that you were there once, yourself. You thought that if you were negative, that you would be able to get the sympathy of others around you. You may not have wanted them to do anything, but what you did want was for them to acknowledge that your life was difficult.

Yet no one knows why they want others to think this about them. They just know that they do, and they will say what they need to in order to get people to feel sorry for them.

But what if I can't bring them up?

Odds are, you won't be able to. Thinking in a positive way is something that each person has to decide for themselves. It isn't anything you can force on anyone, and it isn't anything you can impress on anyone by being around them.

Sure, you have a lot of influence when you are around people, likely more than you know, but you still can only control how you feel about a situation. Each and every person has to decide for themselves whether they want to feel good about something or not.

There are people that really do enjoy feeling sorry for themselves. They don't want to feel better, and they would rather you didn't try to help them. What they want is to feel bad about themselves, and they want you to feel bad for them.

If you fixed it, you would take away their purpose in feeling bad in the first place. What they want is for you to feel bad for them, and for you to think that they are going through a difficult time.

In fact, they may call you things like "annoying," or "thinking you're better than they are," but these are things that you just need to let roll off your back. There is nothing you can do to make them change their minds, and people are going to think what they want to think, regardless of what you tell them.

If you are a positive person, that makes you different than they are, and that is something that they want to be negative about. To the negative person, there can't be anything that is different, and there can't be anyone that is positive about it.

The more you are positive, the more they are seeing that you can be, and the more they think that they need to be that way, too, but it seems hard to get there, and it doesn't feel as good to them as being negative does.

Be that ray of sunshine to the world, and let the clouds be the clouds.

There are all kinds of phrases that talk about haters and nay sayers, and there is a strand of truth to them. You can still choose to be that ray of sunshine or positivity, no matter what other people are saying.

You will feel better about life if you do, and you will soon find that there is no way for them to change how you feel. You may be lucky enough to pull some other people to your way of thinking, but even if you don't, that's ok, too.

Happiness and positivity are very personal things, you will feel it whether everyone else does, or if nobody else does... it is something that comes from within. Once you are able to realize this, and apply it to your own life, you will see that being positive isn't all that hard after all.

Let's take a look at this topic from a new angle, and you will get a better perspective on how you can be positive even if everyone else is negative.

Puppies. Think about them for a second. Now, don't go thinking about all of the fine details or how much you want one, think about their attitudes in life.

They go through their day, they play with the other puppies, and if they get scolded by their mother, they just keep going. You don't see a puppy refusing to have a good day because it got in trouble, or even if you see a puppy that has to be in a crate all day, see how excited it gets to go for a walk.

There are aspects about the puppy's life that makes us think that we wouldn't be so happy if we were in the same situation as the puppy, but if you look at the dog, you will notice that the dog doesn't seem to be phased by how his day is going.

Sure, he may have had to be in his kennel all day, but he still is wagging his tail when he sees his human at the end of the day, even if it is only for a few moments.

We need to get this kind of attitude in our own lives. Sure, there are things that need to be treated with a lot more care than a puppy gives them, but what I am talking about is the overall attitude. Don't assume that your life is over just because something didn't go your way.

Don't focus on the fact that you were in a crate all day and you only got to go for a 30 minute walk. You get out there and you take in that walk for everything that it is, and you enjoy each and every little thing that walk has to offer you.

You will find that life itself doesn't seem so heavy if you treat it this way, and you are going to be able to cope with life in a much more positive manner.

Not everything is going to go your way all of the time. There are few people that get their way all the time, and you may have noticed that those people aren't very happy anyway.

Embrace life for what it is and what you have in it. Not material possessions, but with your life itself. You have such a beautiful opportunity on this planet, and you are given so much to enjoy that is so easy to let slip by.

People on this planet are negative. That is a fact that we all are aware of, and we all have to live with. Sure, it would be nice if we could change everyone, but we can only change ourselves, so why worry about it?

It really doesn't matter what anyone else says or does, or how they are feeling. Sure, you think that if they were happy, then they would be better off, just like you, but then you realize that they don't want to positive, and you have to just let that be.

You can be positive, even if no one else in the whole world is. When you are the one who is being positive, then you are feeling good about yourself, and that is what is important. If anyone else wants to be positive and feel good about themselves, that is their choice.

It isn't up to you to make anyone else happy in this world. Happiness is a personal choice, and it is one that everyone needs to make for themselves.

Chapter 5 – Science behind the Practice

Now, we could pass this all off as fact, when without science, it is really a matter of opinion. Thankfully, there really is science to back up the whole matter of thinking positively, and how it affects your outlook on life.

Since 1985, scientists have been studying the positive effects that thinking positively has on the human body. It does all kinds of things, from lessening loneliness, to making pain tolerance go up.

Optimistic people are more likely to make and keep friends, although they are also less likely to feel the need to have friends. They excel at work, and they come up with better ideas for the company.

Although it doesn't seem likely there are a lot of literal, physical effects that come from thinking positively. People have been known to handle treatments for different illnesses better, and some have even been reported to completely get over whatever illness was plaguing them.

You may have noticed in your own life that you are sleeping better, and that you are feeling better about life in general in the times when you feel that everything is going well.

You assume that things are looking up, and that they are going to keep looking up. This is an attitude that affects your whole life, and it shows. You are better able to get up and go to work, you are better able to get your job done with fewer mistakes.

You eat healthier, you sleep better, you have more energy all through the day. Nothing is really different in your life besides your attitude, and your outlook.

Now, it doesn't matter if things are going to fall apart eventually. When you are in this state you don't even think about what happens when they do. It goes beyond being prepared. Sure, you need to be ready for things as they happen, but being ready doesn't mean that you are always dreading what could happen.

You know that things happen, but you have an attitude that tells you that it will be ok if it does. You know that you are able to handle it, and you don't stress. This is why you are so energetic, and you are able to cope with life so well.

A person with a negative outlook isn't going to have so good of an attitude about life, they are so worried about when something bad is going to happen, they don't even think about how good they have it right now.

That is why they have such positive affects showing on their physical being. They aren't worried about what is going to happen next, even though they are ready for it when it does, and it shows.

There really is no definite limit to how thinking this way can help you, but it is certain that it does. What makes it even better is that positive thinking is not something that comes out based on circumstances.

People can be perfectly happy and perfectly positive no matter what their circumstances really is, as this is a thought process that comes from within. In one study, it was even revealed that it was the less fortunate people, and the people that were struggling with different illnesses that were the happiest of all.

It was the rich people and the people who were considered to be better off that were the ones who were not as happy, or who were more likely to gripe about their circumstances, and, as a result, these were the people that were also less healthy, and had more problems in life all around.

There are all kinds of theories as to why people are happier, or think more positively than other people, whether they are in the same situation or not, but what ultimately prevails is the fact that it is by choice.

All too often we hear someone say "they made me feel this way," or "I wouldn't have done that, but they made me." In all honesty, this is just a way to evade taking responsibility, and to push the blame on someone else.

We are in charge of our own feelings. As human beings, we are designed to take care of things ourselves. Our brains are wired to like company and enjoy companionship, but when it comes to dealing with things, we are entirely on our own in that.

This is why it is possible for two people who go through the same exact set of circumstances to have such drastic differences when it comes to how they react. You see it in the case of tragedy, such as a divorce or when parents lose a child.

One may seem to be handling the situation really well, while the other one is withering away into nothingness. Or, they both may be doing fine, or they both may be struggling. What is really happening here is how they are dealing with the situation in their own minds.

Sure, they may have the same support system, or they may have entirely different support systems. Some people may require the company of a lot of supporters, others prefer to be left completely alone to deal with whatever is happening.

No matter what the situation is, what is important here is to realize that how you feel about something has nothing to do with the circumstance you are going through, or what other people in the situation are telling you.

Outside circumstances can't make you feel one way or another, and neither can another person. No matter what another person says or does, no matter how they try to make you feel, there isn't a thing another person on this planet can tell you that will make you feel any way.

Chapter 6 – The 'What if' Factor

A lot of people out there start their day with every intention to be positive. They get up, get ready for the day, and head out their doors with a smile on their face and head off to work.

Then, without warning, they have a though. It isn't a bad thought, but it isn't a good thought, either. In and of itself, it is just a thought, but it is one that sets the tone for their entire day, and the tone isn't one that is very good.

So what is that thought? Well, nothing to make mention of, in fact, they don't know themselves if it is going to happen, they just wonder 'what if it does?'

I am now going to discuss with you the 'what if' factor, and the horribly damaging roll it plays on society as we know it. There doesn't have to be anything happening to us or in our days, and this factor can ruin our days, or put us in such a bad mood that we may as well have had our day ruined.

It is the same idea as being a worrier, and we all know how hard it is to overcome worry. There doesn't have to be any basis for what they are thinking, or what they are afraid of, the fact that it could happen is enough to dampen their moods, and throw them into the path of negativity.

What makes this all even harder to overcome is the fact that there isn't anything in particular you can do about it in advance. The what if factor is one that is the effect of many years of negativity, and it is defeated through many weeks of positivity.

When you get stuck in the thinking of what could possibly happen, verses what really is happening, you are doing what is known as 'borrowing trouble'. Now, I don't need to tell you that you already have enough trouble on your own that you don't need to go borrowing it, but that won't stop you from worrying.

You don't even know if what you are worried about will come true, and in the long run, it doesn't really matter if it does or doesn't. Worrying about whether or not it could happen tends to be enough to keep you busy, even if it doesn't happen, at least until you have something new to worry about.

So how do I overcome this 'what if' thinking? I am having a hard enough time trying to get positive, and this seems to make it sound even harder to get there.

I am not going to tell you that it is going to be easy, but what I will tell you is that it is possible, and you are able to do it without much problem at all.

To get over this factor, you need to retrain your thoughts. While that is the sole purpose of what we are working on anyway, there is a bit of a different method here.

Instead of changing all of your thoughts to happy thoughts of butterflies and flowers, you need to stop thinking about the 'what if's altogether. If you are familiar with the concept of fate, then you know that you can't change anything that is going to happen anyway, and worrying about it only makes it worse.

You need to enjoy your life for what it is, and not for what you fear will happen, or what you wish it was. You have been given everything that you need in this life, and you should be happy. If you are stuck in the thinking that you are going to lose it all, or worried that you might, then you would be better off enjoying it now while you still had it.

The positive thinker knows that this life is passing. They understand that each and every moment is a gift, and that we are here to enjoy what we have. It is a lot better to not know or worry about what is going to happen next, as that will take away from the beauty of the moment that is happening right now.

It really does help for you to imagine that every moment is your last. Some people argue that is a bleak way to look at life, but I ask you, is it really?

If you don't know when your last moment will be, then won't you enjoy what moments you have all the more? For some, the answer is yes, for others, the answer is no, but I challenge you to think about the answer to this question in your own life.

Would you really want to know when your last moment was? And if so, why? What difference does it make today if it is your last day, or if it won't be your last day for another hundred years?

Each day has been created for our enjoyment, and you should be out there enjoying yours. Be happy that you are able to see it, and think of all the beauty that it has to offer. Don't think about yesterday, and don't think about tomorrow, only think about today.

If you struggle with the 'what if' factor, then I challenge you to only think about right now. Don't think about 5 minutes ago, and don't think of what will happen 5 minutes from now. All you have is this moment right now, and it is beautiful.

The more you learn to live in the moment, the less you are going to worry about what might or might not happen tomorrow. You will learn that there is beauty in the present time, and that there is a lot to be had here and now.

This thinking alone will bring you closer to your goal of being a positive person, and after a very short amount of time, you are going to be amazed at how easy it comes to you.

So don't worry or even think about what could happen tomorrow, you are here, today, and right now, so enjoy it for everything that it is.

Chapter 7 – Looking in the Mirror

Thinking you are a positive person and actually being one are two very different things. There are many people on this planet that think they are the lights of their own lives, but in actuality, they are some of the biggest contributors to their own negativity.

We love to point out in others the things that we are either jealous of, or the things that we don't like about ourselves. This is pretty ironic, and you may deny it to yourself, but it is true, and if you really examine yourself, you will see that it is.

But why? Wouldn't we rather pick on them for things that we don't like about them? Or things that we really do wish they would change? Wouldn't we feel better about ourselves if we did the same thing?

Our minds are funny things. We think we do what we want to do a lot of the time, but we really do what we feel like we should be doing, at least that is how a lot of us cope with life.

There really are few people that do what they want in their lives, and those few people still seem to gravitate towards the negative. They hang out with others who are negative, the only thing that seems to come out of their mouth is negativity, and they only think about things that are negative.

Yet, all the while, they are talking about those people they know who are negative, and telling other people that they wish the world was a better place!

As much as we hate to admit it, we are responsible for a lot of the negativity in this world, and it is our own attitudes that breeds more negativity. Even if we say that we want it to be a brighter and cheerier place to be, we still tend to gravitate and focus on the negative things in our lives.

But if we are the negative ones, wouldn't we realize that we are the ones causing the problem?

Not necessarily, actually. As we have said before, we as people tend to gripe about and harp on those things that we dislike in ourselves, even if we don't realize that we do it ourselves. This is especially true when it comes to things that affects others besides just us.

Don't be discouraged, however, there is hope for you, and everyone else in this quest to end negativity. It will take practice, admission, and a willingness to change your own way of thinking, but you still can do it, you just have to get out there and make yourself do it.

But how can I change something that I don't see in myself?

That is another good question, but the answer is simple. Just because you don't see it in yourself right off the bat, doesn't mean that it isn't there, or that you can't change it if you try.

The first part of this problem is to identify that you have the problem, and that you can change it. Take a minute to think about yourself, how you feel about things, what you tend to think about, and your general attitude in life.

It is important to note that we are not saying that you are wrong, or that you are a bad person, we are genuinely trying to help you overcome this bad habit, and move forward with your life. The best way to examine yourself, is to keep an eye on your interactions, or to genuinely assess how you are thinking about things.

If you choose to go with the first manner of learning, then you need to pay close attention to your day, from the beginning to the end. We have encouraged you to look at your day in earlier chapters, and to figure out where the negativity is creeping in.

Now, I want you to analyze again, and see where you are contributing the negativity. This is a hard thing to do, especially when you are not entirely sure that you are part of the problem. That, of course, is a pretty simple concept to grasp, after all, no one wants to admit that they are part of any problem.

So what are you going to do? How are you going to identify what you need to do to stop this bad habit, and how are you going to determine if you really do have it?

Well, let me save you some time and effort here. This is a book that is talking about how you can break out of this negativity in your life, and embrace a more positive outlook. It doesn't take a rocket scientist here to figure out that you already know that you have a problem with negativity, otherwise you probably wouldn't have picked up this book.

So, with that out of the way, let's take this a step further, and determine why you have a problem. We already know that the problem is there; which is going to take off a lot of pressure later on, trust me. So let's look at why it is there.

We can blame society, or we can look on the inside. Of course it is a lot easier to say that we are a product of what we are around, or we can say that it isn't our fault, and that we should just do our best in this world that we live in.

I want to remind you, however, that there are a lot of people that live in society, that are not like society. Sure, we are not going to focus on what other people are doing, that is why I am encouraging you to look inside of yourself, but at the same time, it is important to know that I am not asking the impossible.

Chapter 8 – Going against the Grain: Standing out in Society

It is really easy to point out that the rest of the world is wrong, or to sit back and point the finger at the other people in our lives, and say how we wished they were more positive, or better able to control that negativity.

Where this gets difficult is when we decide to look inside ourselves, and see where we fit in this big realm of positivity. As we have already said, it is really easy to point that finger outward, but what about on the inside? Where do we fall on that scale of negativity?

In the last chapter, we took a look at the plain and simple fact, you have a personal problem with negative thinking. Now that may sound harsh when I put it bluntly, but the fact of the matter is that it doesn't matter to you whether or not I have a problem with negativity, or if anyone else on this planet does.

What matters is that you do, and we are going to find a way to get you out of that habit, and into a much healthier one. As we have said at the beginning of this chapter, it is really easy to point the finger at others and claim they are the reason we are negative, but then again, we need to look deeper, and realize that is not possible.

Think of it this way, if everyone on the planet woke up tomorrow, and started eating stink bugs for every meal, you would not start to eat stink bugs for the plain and simple fact everyone else was doing it.

To make my point even more clear, just because everyone else is doing it doesn't make the idea of eating a stink bug any more appealing to you, in fact, it likely still grosses you out... possibly even more because everyone else is doing it.

So, by that plain and simple analogy, you know that you don't have to do something just because everyone else is doing it, and you don't even have to care what they have to say about you not joining in.

Negativity is the same way. Yes, it is a habit, and a bad one at that, but that doesn't mean that you should do it, or that you should find any appeal in doing it because that is what the rest of the world is doing.

Think of each and every negative comment you hear as a stink bug, and think about how gross it is to put that in your mouth. In the same way, you don't want to put that nasty negativity in or out of your mouth, no matter who is doing it.

Ok, I don't want to do it anymore, but it isn't as easy as turning off a light switch now, is it?

Right you are. That is what I meant when I pointed out that this is a habit. Now, this isn't new information. In the earlier parts of this book, we examined how this is a habit, and that it needs to be broken, but we didn't go too far into doing what works for you, or what you can do that will make it that much easier for you to break out of this negativity and pick up on the positive.

Step 1: replace it.

Anyone who has quit a bad habit in their life will tell you one simple fact... they didn't just stop that bad habit, they replaced it with something good. You may want to just snap your fingers and have it all be over with, but that isn't how our bodies work, and it isn't how our minds are designed.

No matter what you are doing with your day, you have to fill that time with something. Most people tend to get up, go to work, go do something else with the rest of their day, then go home and go to bed.

If they decide that they want to do something different, they still have that same amount of time that needs to be filled in their day, they just need to fill it with something that they weren't doing before. This is the same with any bad habit.

If you want to quit smoking, most people pick up on chewing gum instead. If you want to quit drinking, most people pick another beverage or some sort of hobby instead. Sure, there are still hours that need to be used, but those hours don't need to be used in a bad habit.

So what do I replace negativity with?

The short and simple (and I dare say, obvious) answer is to replace it with positivity. Of course to someone who is in the midst of a bad habit, simply telling them to replace negativity with positivity is as about as effective as telling a sheepdog to simply not herd sheep.

You need to think for a few minutes, and think about something that you like. Now, you can't always replace an activity with an activity, but you can replace a subject matter pretty easily. What I mean by that is that you have to go to work, and you have to see the same people you see every day.

If they are expecting you to be negative, they are likely going to try to be negative when they see you. Now, this isn't your fault. They are likely negative people anyway, and you are just a convenient person to be negative with.

My point is that you can't quit your job because you don't want to be negative anymore, but what you can do is find something new to talk about. If you like sports, beat them to the chase with the topic.

If you sense that the topic is going somewhere negative, then turn it around with a topic that you do like. There isn't anything wrong with keeping the subject matter on things that you like, or that you are doing in your life, as long as it is staying away from the negative.

And who knows? Maybe with your new attitude, and your new way of speech, you might influence someone else to join in your positivity, and you are going to see an improvement in the situation all around. Now, this may not happen, or you may only find one or two people to talk to, but that is better than gossiping and complaining with a group of people.

Remember, this is a habit that you are breaking, and that means it is going to take time. You can see some results right away, but there are things that are going to take patience and practice within yourself. Don't get upset if you slip up, you can always do better next time.

Just make sure that there is a next time, and that you are making an effort to do better. All too often people get caught up in the thinking that they have screwed up, and that it is all over for them now, but that is negativity in itself.

Pick yourself up, dust off that bad attitude, and get back in the game. It doesn't matter if you slipped up, you can do better the very next time you say something, and you are going to find that the single conversations will grow into days of positivity, and the days become weeks become years.

Without even realizing it you are going to get that life that you have always wanted to have, and you don't need to stress about how long it has been, or how well you are doing.

Positivity is one that sees the best in people, including yourself. That means that you know and understand that you are human, and that you cut yourself slack, even if no one else is. Be kind to others, and be kind to yourself.

That is the best way to grow this attitude of positivity, and you will be shocked at how well it all spreads.

Chapter 9 – Positivity for Life

Thinking positively isn't something that you do for a while, then stop doing. Positive thinking is a way of life. You have to take the time to make it a habit for yourself, then you have to make a deliberate choice to follow that habit every day.

Some days are going to be easier than others. This is true no matter what it is you are trying to change in your life. If you are on a diet, there are going to be days that you feel great about your diet, and days that you wish you could just break down and eat anything and everything.

The same thing is going to happen to you in your thinking. There are going to be days when you feel great, and when everything is going just right. These days are great, they make you feel like you can do this all the time, no matter what happens.

Then there are the days that aren't so great. The days when everything goes wrong, and when you feel that you don't know what you are going to be able to do to make things work out. No matter what you think you can try, you don't see any way for it to turn out ok.

These are the days when you need to make sure that you are doing your part to make this positive thinking a choice, and you have to put that choice into action. Sure, it might be hard, but it isn't going to be as hard as it sounds, especially if you are making all of this a habit of life.

Even when you are in your darkest hour, you still have the choice to be a positive person. Note that I didn't say that you have to always be happy, or that you can't feel stress, but you must maintain that attitude that you are going to make it through this, and that it will all be ok.

I want you to know that we can feel for you, and that you are not alone in this life. For those especially who are going through something, it is hard to hear that you need to be positive.

It is even harder to hear that there are so few positive people out there that you are already pretty alone in this. You are not alone, however, and no matter what you are going through, you are going to make it through.

While there isn't anything wrong with loners, or those that prefer their own company, there also isn't anything wrong with friends, and it is important for you to have your support system. Even if it is one that is shaky, you need to understand that you are strong, and that you are never alone in anything.

Positivity is an attitude, but it is one that is better developed by those that are able to be ok alone, but are also able to recognize that they are not alone. This is a huge planet that we live on, and even if you seem to be alone in a situation, you aren't.

There is someone, somewhere, who can relate to you and knows what you are going through. Sure, you may not know them personally, and you may never meet them, but they are there, and you are not the only one who is going through this.

If you were able to talk to them, you would hear for yourself that they are there for you, and no matter what happens next, you are going to be ok. Never undermine the fact that it is worth the world to hear that you are going to be ok.

And that is one of the major things that positive people are about. They know that there are tough times, but they don't worry about those, they are thinking of the time when they know they are going to be ok.

Sure, it may take a while to get there, and they may know it for themselves, in fact, there are those that are suffering from illness or disease, and they know that they will not be able to get better, but they are still positive, because they know that they are going to be ok no matter what happens, and that their families are going to be ok as well.

You are a strong enough person to make this all happen, and if you believe that is so, you are already embracing a form of positive thinking, you do have influence in society, and there are all kinds of things you can say and do that will help other people see things as you do.

Now, I'm not saying you are always going to be some bubbly positive person. There are definitely going to be times when you feel down, or when you need someone to come build up your spirits, but if you make this your habit of life, you are going to see the long term results.

All in all things aren't going to seem like they are that crushing, and you will always be able to find the good in a situation. It can be hard, especially when you are surrounded by people that don't agree with positive thinking, but don't worry, as we saw in the last chapter, you don't have to be influenced by what is going on around you.

You can be perfectly happy, even if everyone else is being pessimistic and finding fault in things. But, as we have also seen before, it doesn't take much for that to be reversed.

Don't be afraid to be that person who is different, to be the one that has a cause, and the one that is willing to see the light in things. You may not notice that other people are admiring you, but you may notice that there aren't many people that say bad things about a positive person.

The truth of the matter is that these people you are around are going to admire you for your positivity, and that they would like to have that same level of positivity in their own lives.

All you have to do is set your mind to it, and you can be the positive person in any situation. You will be surprised at how easy this is when you are in practice, it just takes a bit of time to get there.

Remember though, you can think positively about this whole process. There are few things that are more counter-productive than criticizing yourself for not thinking positively. The whole point of this is to make you feel better about yourself, and to feel better all around.

Practice makes perfect, and practice is progress. The more you work at it, the better it is going to be, and the easier it will come to you. Don't let anyone tell you that you are annoying, or that you need to feel sorry for yourself like the rest of the world does.

You are your own human, and that in itself is a miracle. Don't let anyone or anything define you besides your own self. You are on top of your game, now get out there and rock the world.

Conclusion

Thank you again for downloading this book!

I hope this book was able to help you to realize that there is a lot of good in life, even when it might be hiding behind a cloud of doubt.

The next step is to practice and persevere. There is nothing that is able to make you change how you feel, and you will find that the more positive you are about a situation, the less bad it seems to be.

There will be some hard days to go through, but you will find that those days will get fewer and further between the more positively you think. It is a reaction that builds upon itself, and the more you feed it, the more you will feel it.

Few things are more contagious then positivity, so be the beacon this world needs. Don't be afraid to be the only person in a room who is seeing the positive in a situation, it may be hard for others to join in at first, but if you are consistent, you will see that you can make a real difference to those around you!

Finally, if you enjoyed this book, then I'd like to ask you for a favor, would you be kind enough to leave a review for this book on Amazon? It'd be greatly appreciated!

Visit:

http://www.amazon.com/Positive-Thinking-Negative-Happiness-Psychology-ebook/dp/B014P7D654

To leave a review for this book on Amazon!

Do not forget to visit this website: ProjectSuperPerformance.com! Free and fantastic content about super performance. For example: How to lose weight, how to study 14 hours in one day and much more.

At the moment you can get a free copy of

"33.5 Power Habits"!

Go and get it now!! At: www.ProjectSuperPerformance.com

Also! If you enjoyed this book check my other book named:

"*How To Be Happy Alone*" Buy it by visiting:

http://www.amazon.com/How-Be-Happy-Confident-Happiness-ebook/dp/B00XT7RPTA

Or see the preview on next page.

Thank you and good luck!

Preview from "How to Be Happy Alone"

I want to thank you and congratulate you for downloading the book, "*How to be Happy Alone*".

This book contains proven steps and strategies on how to find happiness even though you're single. It is a common misconception in the world we live in that we need to have a significant other in order to be happy.

Society tells us that we need to have that person to go to in the good times and the bad times, have that person to snuggle up with at night, and have that person to help with the bills and to be that person who is always blowing up your phone with cute little messages.

Or, if you are not having a significant other for the sake of your own satisfaction, society tells us to have one in order to prove to everyone that we can 'get' one. There is almost an unspoken mark of failure placed on singles, as though there is something wrong with them for not having a boyfriend or girlfriend.

Then, of course, comes the dreaded Valentine's Day. The stupid holiday that society has dreamt up that basically forces us to have significant others, otherwise risk enduring twenty-four hours of pity and single shaming by those who do have boyfriends or girlfriends.

This holiday has affected us so much that we have actually created apps to message us throughout the day and play the part of a significant other, just to look to the rest of the world as though we have one, or to make ourselves feel better about the fact that we do not.

That, my friend, is not how we were designed to be. Don't get me wrong, there is nothing wrong with having that other person, and there is nothing at all wrong with the cute messages, and the fun times you have together, or anything like that.

What I want to make clear is that while those things are all fun and good, they are not necessary for you to be happy. You do not need to have another person to be the happiest person on the planet, and there is no significant other that you can have that will make anyone think any more of you than they do right now.

You are all the validation that you need to be happy with yourself, and you are enough all on your own to show the rest of the world what you are made of. Just because you feel that you look better when you have someone hanging off your arm, you really don't.

"But I can't be alone," you say, or, "I don't want to die alone." A feeling that drives a lot of people to have relationship after relationship, even when they are not happy in them, or they don't like the person they are partnering with.

There is a truth, however, that may change how you feel about those statements, and that is the fact no one can make you feel any more or less alone than you are right now. At the end of the day, when you sleep, you are asleep alone, even if you are snuggled against someone.

While we are designed to want and like companionship, there are many ways we can get that without being in a relationship. It is a complete myth that you need someone else to be happy, true happiness comes from within.

In this book we are going to look at how you can become happy all on your own, whether you are currently in a relationship or not. You will see that it doesn't matter who you are, what you do for a living, or how much money you make, you will learn what it is like to be truly happy, and yet be entirely single.

Now, if you are currently in a relationship, I am not going to tell you to break up with your significant other, and if you are single, I am not going to tell you that you need to be opposed to a relationship.

What I am going to tell you is that you cannot possibly be happy in a relationship unless you are already happy on your own, and by going through this book you are going to learn how to be happy with you, just as you are, right now.

You will learn a new and amazing way of life. One that will enhance the relationship you are in if you have one, or a fact that will make you receptive to a relationship, but not make that be your goal.

You will find that you can be happier than you ever thought possible, and that it all comes from within. You won't have to spend a dime, or make any drastic change to your life, you are just going to learn simple little tips and tricks that will show you how to be happy, right here, and right now.

The only one who can make you happy, is you, and the only one who is standing in the way of that happiness is you. There is nothing on this planet that can touch that, and you are about to discover how to be happy alone.

What are you waiting for? There is a life out there that is waiting for you to live it. Don't waste another second waiting for that Mr. or Mrs. Right to come along, you are your own Right, and you have a life to live.

Thanks again for downloading this book, I hope you enjoy it!

Read More by visiting:

http://www.amazon.com/How-Be-Happy-Confident-Happiness-ebook/dp/B00XT7RPTA

And again! If you enjoyed "*Positive Thinking*" I would love to read your review. Leave yours at by visiting:

http://www.amazon.com/Positive-Thinking-Negative-Happiness-Psychology-ebook/dp/B014P7D654

Thank You!

CPSIA information can be obtained
at www.ICGtesting.com
Printed in the USA
LVOW04s0759280116

472523LV00031BA/1246/P